Medical English Word Partnerships 1 Workbook

By

James Hugh Stevenson

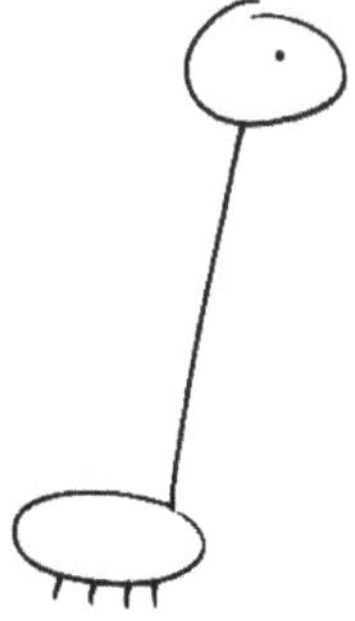

Premier Potential Publishing

Medical English Word Partnerships 1
Workbook

Published by Premier Potential Publishing
プレミア ポテンシャル パブリッシング

premierpotentialpublishing@gmail.com
www.premierpotentialpublishing.com

Front and Back Cover Design: rebecacovers

ISBN: 978-4-9910600-5-2
First Print Edition

Table of Contents

Acknowledgements

The author would like to thank his wife, family and friends for their love and support.
In addition, the author would like to thank his English students in Asahikawa, Japan. They are the inspiration behind this book. Special thanks go to the English language students at the Red Cross Hospital in Asahikawa.

About the author

James Hugh Stevenson has been teaching English in Japan for over eleven years. He lives with his wife in Asahikawa, Japan. James has a lot of experience in teaching English. He has taught adults and children. James currently teaches English at a private high school, at the Red Cross Hospital in Asahikawa, to individuals and at private businesses in Asahikawa, Japan.

Introduction

This textbook is designed for English language learners who want to improve their medical English.
This book will improve English language learner's vocabulary. Learners will be able to understand how to use common, natural English to explain medical situations and problems in simple English.
Each unit has ten exercises of varying difficulty. Students will learn vocabulary and practice using it in sentences. There is a focus on asking and answering questions related to working in the medical industry.

10% Red Cross Donation

The author will donate 10% of his personal profits to the Japanese Red Cross to help support their good work.

How to use this textbook

Students should complete the exercises and then check the answers.
Answers can be found online at www.premierpotentialpublishing.com and at the back of this book.

Take a break.

Take

Examples

Take advice
You should take the doctor's advice.
Take medicine
You need to take this medicine.
Take a rest
You look exhausted. You need to take a rest.
Take a break
I'm going to take a break for five minutes.
Take a bath/shower
I'm filthy. Can I take a bath?

Take a seat
Please, take a seat.
Take a test/exam
You need to take an eye exam.
Take care
Take care of yourself.
Take a picture/an x-ray
We need to take an x-ray of your chest.
Take responsibility
You must take responsibility for your weight.

Exercise 1

Make a list of other medical collocations of ***take***.

Exercise 2

Unscramble the words.

1. I'm going to take **oyu** ***you*** to the operating room.
2. You look tired. You should take a **kebra** _______________.
3. Take two **lttabes** _______________three times a day after meals.
4. He hasn't taken a **hatb** _______________for three months. He is very dirty!
5. I'm not going to take **ionsiertylspib** _______________for that. It's not my fault.
6. I took a **xtai** _______________ to the hospital.
7. Bob hasn't taken a **oehswr** _______________ for two weeks. He is quite smelly.
8. I gave up my job to take **rcae** _______________of my elderly mother.
9. Nurse, please take Mr. Johnson's **etremerpatu** _______________.
10. I'm afraid he has been taking illegal **rdusg** _______________.

Exercise 3

Match the beginning of the sentences on the left with the correct ending on the right.

1. Take aspirin __F__
2. Take a vacation _____
3. Take care _____
4. Take a taxi _____
5. Take some blood _____
6. Take an x-ray _____
7. Take my advice _____
8. Take a few days _____
9. Take a class _____
10. Take your time _____

A. of your health.
B. off work.
C. of his chest.
D. to the hospital.
E. from the patient.
F. for a headache.
G. in first aid.
H. and quit smoking.
I. to Hawaii.
J. there is no hurry.

Exercise 4

Write the missing words in the blank spaces.

medication / care / for granted / pharmacy / anything / ~~**seat**~~ / vacation / one pill a day / time / yoga / herbal

A: Good morning Mrs Jones. Please take a ***seat***.
B: Thanks.
A: What seems to be the trouble?
B: I've been very tired recently. I just can't seem to sleep.
A: Have you been taking _______________ to help you sleep?
B: Yes, I've been taking over the counter herbal _______________, but it hasn't been working.
A: Have you had any stress in your life recently?
B: Yes, both at home and at work. I think my husband has been taking me _______________. I can't do everything.
A: I see. You sound very busy. Maybe your trouble sleeping is down to stress. Can you take a short _______________, just by yourself?
B: No way, I've got too much to do?
A: Okay, well let me give you a prescription for some sleeping pills. Take it to the_______________. Only take a maximum of _______________. Do not take more than that. Stop taking the _______________ medication. Don't take both at the same time.
B: I understand.
A: If possible, take some _______________ for yourself every day. Maybe take up_______________.
B: Thank you doctor.
A: You're welcome. Take_______________.

Exercise 5

Cross out the words that do **NOT** collocate with ***take***.

1.	medicine	a pill	a tablet	~~antiseptic cream~~
2.	your time	a break	sleep	a nap
3.	through	down	up	out
4.	a day off	a holiday	time off	free time
5.	a phone	a call	a message	advice
6.	a shower	a toilet	a bath	a wet tissue
7.	foot	a bus	an ambulance	a taxi
8.	care	after	a see	advantage
9.	off	on	at	in
10.	a blood test	an x-ray	a heart review	an eye exam

Exercise 6

Number the sentences to make a conversation. Which sentences are said by the doctor and which are said by the patient? Write **D** for doctor and **P** for patient.

_____Thank you.
_____I will. Thanks again.
_____What seems to be the trouble?
_____I've had a headache for the past five days.
D 1 Hello, please take a seat.
_____Here is a prescription for some stronger pain killers. Only take two every four hours. These pills can take about ten minutes to take effect.
_____Thank you, doctor.
_____Have you taken anything for it?
_____Take my advice and take a rest.
_____I've been taking aspirin, but it hasn't worked.

Exercise 7

Read the passage, then answer the questions.

Man taken to hospital after taking too much heroin.

A man in his early twenties was found unconscious on Pine Street in the early hours of Sunday morning. He was taken by ambulance to hospital. The emergency room doctors stabilized him, and he is now recovering in hospital. The doctors took some blood and it was discovered that he had taken an overdose of heroin. Police are not sure if he intended to take his own life. The police said that he is an escaped prisoner. He escaped by assaulting a guard and taking his uniform and keys. He is a conman who used to take advantage of the elderly and take their money. He will be taken back to prison as soon as he recovers.

1. Why is the man in hospital?
He had taken an overdose of drugs.
2. What kind of drugs had he taken?
____
3. What did the doctors take from the patient?
____
4. How did he escape from prison.
____
5. Why was the man in prison?
____

Exercise 8

What do the following sentences mean?

1. I can't take it anymore!

   ____

2. He can't take a joke.

   ____

Exercise 9

Write medical sentences using ***take***.

____

____

____

____

____

Exercise 10

Answer the questions.

1. What do you always take on vacation?

____

____

2. Why might a doctor need to take blood from a patient?

____

____

3. Do you take supplements?

____

____

4. Who do you take after?

____

____

5. What did you take from this lesson?

____

____

Don’t give up!

Give

Examples

Give advice

The doctor gave me some good advice.

Give permission

We need the parent’s permission.

Give an example

Can you give me an example, please?

Give a headache

Whiskey gives me a headache.

Give a stomachache

I think that fish gave me a stomachache.

Give a cold

The boy with the runny nose gave me his cold.

Give a disease

Please, don’t give me that. I don’t want to get sick.

Give up

Don’t give up, you must keep fighting.

Give news

I don’t like giving bad news to patients.

Give birth

My wife gave birth to our first child last month.

Exercise 1

Make a list of other medical collocations of ***give***.

____

____

____

____

____

____

____

____

____

Exercise 2

Complete the word search.

O	L	S	S	K	Y	V	D	W	E	S	P	P	A	X
H	O	P	E	Q	V	S	Q	F	C	N	V	E	L	J
J	P	S	I	D	D	Z	F	R	H	Z	M	R	N	C
G	I	H	M	S	H	X	G	Y	O	P	L	M	G	O
F	N	T	Y	H	D	A	D	V	I	C	E	I	J	L
R	I	Q	V	K	I	I	O	J	C	X	E	S	Y	D
N	O	B	Q	I	S	V	P	G	E	C	D	S	R	U
M	N	I	W	Y	E	L	L	D	W	N	S	I	W	A
O	Z	R	E	E	A	L	K	H	I	E	A	O	D	R
W	N	T	U	D	S	D	T	F	O	T	K	N	H	Q
Q	M	H	J	H	E	S	G	L	Y	S	L	A	A	F
F	X	P	Y	K	R	T	M	E	D	I	C	I	N	E
D	R	F	D	L	L	H	Y	O	G	D	I	E	D	D
I	T	E	P	O	J	I	T	O	G	B	E	E	H	O
P	R	I	O	R	I	T	Y	E	X	A	M	P	L	E

advice / ~~birth~~ / choice / cold / disease / example / hand / hope / medicine / opinion / permission / priority

Exercise 3

Unscramble the words. The first letter has been done for you.

1. mtie **time**
2. hcicoe c _ _ _ _ _
3. urlecte l _ _ _ _ _ _
4. ngri r _ _ _
5. rmesinpios p _ _ _ _ _ _ _ _ _
6. hugohtt t _ _ _ _ _ _
7. ipemrssoin i _ _ _ _ _ _ _ _ _
8. nsaewr a _ _ _ _ _
9. eeencvid e _ _ _ _ _ _ _
10. uhg h _ _

Exercise 4

Write sentences using ***give*** and the words from exercises 2 and 3.

1. <u>I'm sorry, I can't **give** you any more of my time. The hospital is very busy today.</u>
2. ______________________________
3. ______________________________
4. ______________________________
5. ______________________________
6. ______________________________
7. ______________________________
8. ______________________________
9. ______________________________
10. ______________________________

Exercise 5

Write the missing words in the blank spaces.

time / advice / hand / ~~**blood**~~ / stomachache / shock / boost / lift / birth / aspirin

1. Yesterday, I gave <u>**blood**</u>. I'm type A and I donated about a pint.
2. My wife is due to give ______________ next month. I'm nervous about becoming a father.
3. I will never forget the ______________ that my father gave me. He told me to believe in myself.
4. Eating too much ice cream, too quickly usually gives me a ______________.
5. Can you give me some ______________? I have a headache.
6. Those bags look heavy. Can I give you a ______________?
7. The exposed wire gave me an electric ______________.
8. Would you mind giving me a ______________ to the hospital tomorrow?
9. Coffee gives me a ______________ of energy in the morning.
10. Give me some more ______________, I'm very busy.

Exercise 6

Correct the mistakes. There are two mistakes in each sentence.

1. I ~~**giving**~~ my heavily pregnant wife a ride to the hospital hours before she gave ~~**born**~~.
   I gave my heavily pregnant wife a ride to the hospital hours before she gave birth.
2. Give priorities to the patients with the least life-threatening injuries.

   ____
3. Don't give that man any more treats. He is a hypochondriac, there isn't anything fine with him.

   ____
4. Can you give me a hand dropping this patient? He is very light.

   ____
5. The patient's mother was so angry that she giving the doctor a kiss.

   ____
6. The lectured that Doctor Smith gave about parasites is interesting.

   ____
7. I do give a damn about the risks! We must do the operation then.

   ____
8. I decided to start smoked after the doctor gave me some advice.

   ____

Exercise 7

Put the sentences in the correct order. Put the ***highlighted*** words into the correct position in the sentence.

1. I can't ***you give*** any more ***morphine***. You've already had the ***maximum*** dose.
   I can't give you any more morphine. You've already had the maximum dose.
2. I've ***hard*** very ***nothing***. I have ***give*** else to ***tried***.

   ____
3. The medical student didn't ***enough*** himself ***give finish*** to ***time*** his dissertation.

   ____
4. Would you ***give*** me to ***hug you*** a ***like***?

   ____
5. I've ***best*** you the ***can given*** I ***advice***.

   ____
6. I've decided to ***up give*** on my ***divorce*** and file for ***marriage***.

   ____
7. Let's ***death*** our ***give*** and prayers to Mrs Jones after the ***son*** of her ***thoughts***.

   ____

Exercise 8

Replace the **highlighted** words with a ***give*** phrase.

1. I **didn't have** a choice. The doctors wouldn't discharge me from hospital.
   I wasn't given a choice. The doctors wouldn't discharge me from hospital.
2. Can **I have** some more morphine?
   ____
3. Would you like **some help** with your bags?
   ____
4. We need **your consent** to perform the operation on your husband.
   ____
5. Finding out the cause of the disease **is the prime concern**.
   ____
6. **Let's speak on the phone** later.
   ____
7. That loud music is **making my head hurt**.
   ____
8. Why don't you **care**?
   ____
9. I have to **tell** you some bad news about your condition.
   ____.
10. I don't want to **raise your expectations** just yet.
   ____

Exercise 9

Write medical sentences using ***give***.

____

____

____

____

____

Exercise 10

Answer the questions.

1. What is the best piece of advice that you have ever been given?

____

____

2. Have you ever given blood?

____

____

3. What advice can you give someone who wants to learn medical English?

____

____

4. If you were given the choice, which would you choose; love, money or beauty?

____

____

5. What gives you a headache?

____

____

You're doing well.

Do

Examples

Do exercise
You should do regular exercise.

Do work
I have a lot of work to do tomorrow.

Do surgery/an operation
We need to do an operation to save the patient.

Do good
Try doing good for others in your community.

Do harm
Drinking alcohol can do harm to your liver.

Do a task/job
Please, do this for me.

Do a test/tests
We need to do some tests.

Do a report
Have you done that report on healthcare yet?

Do badly
Doctor Sato did quite badly on his USMLE exam.

Do damage
The accident caused terrible damage to his body.

Exercise 1

Make a list of other medical collocations of ***do***.

____

____

____

____

____

____

____

____

____

Exercise 2

Choose A, B or C.

1. I'm overweight I need to do some **A**.

A. exercise

~~B. diet~~

~~C. lose weight~~

2. The doctor told me that he needs to do a __________ test.

A. hair

B. blood

C. nose

3. Don't do __________! You will hurt yourself.

A. that

B. them

C. something

4. Cleaning staff in a hospital have to do a lot of __________.

A. gowns

B. clothes

C. laundry

5. The kind nurse did the patient's __________ for her to help her look and feel better.

A. hair

B. skin

C. eye

6. The pharmaceutical sales rep was pleased he could do __________ with the hospital.

A. works

B. job

C. business

7. Could you do me a big __________ and lend me $1000?

A. hand

B. help

C. favour

Exercise 3

Write the missing word.

1. Companies do this with each other. Do ***business.***

2. Opposite of your worst. Do your _ _ _ _.

3. You don't do this in your free time. Do _ _ _ _.

4. You might do this in your free time, but you won't achieve anything. Do _ _ _ _ _ _ _.

5. Medical researchers do a lot of this to find out how to cure a disease. Do _ _ _ _ _ _ _ _.

6. Smoking does this to your lungs. Do _ _ _ _ _ _.

Exercise 4

Put these sentences in the correct order. The first word has been done for you.

1. The homework student forgot medical his to do.
   The medical student forgot to do his homework.

2. I report do need to medical this.
   I ____

3. Smoking of damage to can do a lot your lungs.
   Smoking ____

4. The patient the bed has wet. We do the laundry need to.
   The ____

5. Can do me you a favour? I with this need some help patient.
   Can ____

6. I'm drinking my best doing to stop.
   I'm ____

Exercise 5

What do these health care professionals do?

1. **Nutritionist**
   A nutritionist creates specialized dietary plans.
2. **Surgeon**
   ____
3. **Physician**
   ____

Exercise 6

Look at the schedules. Answer the questions.

Dr Bob Taylor, a general practitioner.

Monday	Tuesday	Wednesday	Thursday	Friday	Saturday	Sunday
09:30~10:00 Oliver Green appointment	09:00~09:20 Emma Jones appointment			07:00~08:30 breakfast meeting		
	10:00~11:00 meeting	09:45~12:45 medical conference	10:20~11:30 Kyle Miller appointment	10:00~12:00 NHS surgery hours morning	11:00~12:00 Spanish lesson	day off
10:20~11:20 Julia Wilson appointment	11:15~13:30 John Smith appointment		12:00~12:30 Harry Reed appointment			
	15:30~17:00 Peter Peterson appointment	13:00~13:45 lunch	13:05~14:15 Victoria Lopez appointment	14:00~18:00 NHS surgery hours afternoon	15:00~17:00 tennis	
16:10~16:40 David Goldman appointment			15:00~17:00 Mary Anderson appointment			
17:00~18:30 Felix Brown		14:00~17:00 medical conference	17:15~18:15 Jim O'Conner appointment		1900 dinner with Emma	
18:30 dinner with Kate	17:45~18:45 Mrs Rodriguez appointment		20:00 dinner with Sally			

Sally King, a home health aide.

Monday	Tuesday	Wednesday	Thursday	Friday	Saturday	Sunday
08:30~09:00 Mr Scott 12 Green Street	08:20~08:40 Ms. Thompson 2 Oak Place		07:30~09:00 Mr and Mrs O'Brian 85 Main Street		10:30~11:00 Mr Davis 19 Oxford Street	09:00~10:00 Mrs J King 10 Prince Street
10:00~11:00 Mrs Young 19 Pine Avenue	09:00~010:00 Miss Johnson 32 Oak Place		10:00~13:00 Forrest Green Nursing Home		11:40~12:40: Kate Cunningham 41 Church Lane	10:30~12:00 Peter McKean 11 Prince Street
12:00~13:00 James Hall 29 King Street	10:30~11:30 Mr Scott 12 Green Street	day off	afternoon off 1600~1700 hot yoga 20:00 dinner with Bob	day off	13:00~14:00 Lunch dentist appointment	12:15~12:45 Check in on Mrs H Thompson 22 Prince Street
	12:00~13:00 V Sanchez 123 Maple Drive				14:30~15:40 Ms Jane Hill 99 Station Road	
12:00~14:00 Richard Thornton 101 West Drive	13:40~15:00 Lee Jenkins 5 Abbey Road				16:00~16:10 Check in on Mr Rivers 21 Castle Lane	13:30~15:30 Meeting with Dr Simpson West Clinic
15:00~15:45 Steven Cook 10 Queen Avenue						
16:30~18:00 staff meeting	16:30~18:00 staff meeting			16:30~18:00 staff meeting		16:30~18:00 staff meeting

1. What will Bob do at twenty past ten on Monday morning?

2. What will Sally do at half-past one on Sunday?

3. What will Bob do on Friday?

4. What will Sally do on Sunday?

5. What do you think about what Bob is doing on Monday evening, Thursday evening and Saturday evening?

Exercise 7

Make a list of do's and don'ts in a hospital.

Hospital	
DO	**DON'T**
Wash your hands	Disturb patients

Exercise 8

What do these idioms mean?

1. Bend over backwards to do something

____

____

2. Break one's back to do something

____

____

3. Do as I say, not as I do

____

____

4. Do one's head in

____

____

Exercise 9

Write medical sentences using ***do***.

Exercise 10

Answer the questions.

1. What do you do?

2. What do you have a licence to do?

3. What can you do well?

4. What can't you do very well?

5. What does a nurse do?

Don’t take that. Give it back!

Review

Exercise 1

Complete the word search.

G	D	S	R	Z	B	M	U	I	T	J	P	T	H	A
M	E	D	I	C	I	N	E	L	T	S	N	E	W	S
E	X	O	D	U	R	Y	B	W	J	H	O	A	J	C
T	A	K	E	D	T	D	S	B	E	S	T	L	Y	X
J	M	F	T	R	H	A	I	R	H	O	I	R	V	C
K	P	C	J	N	W	W	W	E	D	R	C	A	L	L
P	L	E	S	S	O	N	J	A	E	D	E	X	L	E
Q	E	I	H	M	H	I	X	K	N	S	H	Q	Z	A
A	O	D	O	D	E	O	P	E	R	A	T	I	O	N
N	E	P	W	E	G	J	I	W	O	R	J	W	J	I
S	N	D	E	C	I	S	I	O	N	U	L	K	X	N
W	N	H	R	G	V	G	N	L	S	R	E	H	U	G
E	W	D	C	E	E	E	K	F	G	T	T	O	D	O
R	D	H	R	B	T	X	E	T	H	Y	Z	P	Q	U
X	U	S	T	O	M	A	C	H	A	C	H	E	C	J

answer / best / birth / break / call / cleaning / decision / do / example / give / hair / hope / hug / lesson ~~medicine~~ / news / notice / operation / ride / shower / stomachache / take

Exercise 2

Write the words in the table. Some words might have more than one correct answer.

~~advice~~ / answer / better / birth / blood / break / care / choice / credit / damage / exercise / harm
headache / housework / laundry / maximum / medicine / notes / paperwork / permission / priority
research / rest / responsibility / right thing / someone's temperature / stomachache / sums / time

Take	Give	Do
advice	advice	

Exercise 3

Match the phrasal verbs on the left with the correct definition on the right.

1. Take off__D__
2. Take on_____
3. Take to_____
4. Take it out on somebody_____
5. Give in_____
6. Give something off_____
7. Give something up_____
8. Do without something_____
9. Do in_____
10. Do with_____

A. want or wish for something
B. hire someone
C. behave badly towards someone because you feel bad
D. to leave
E. to start liking
F. quit or stop doing something
G. give out a bad smell
H. surrender
I. manage without something
J. kill

Exercise 4

Give me some advice on how to improve my medical English.

____

____

Exercise 5

Write ten medical sentences using the phrasal verbs from exercise 3.

Example

The wound is giving off a foul odour. The smell might be caused by bacteria.

1.____

2.____

3.____

4.____

5.____

6.____

7.____

8.____

9.____

10.____

Exercise 6

Write the missing words with the correct form of ***do***, ***give*** or ***take*** in the paragraph.

Jim is a nurse. He always ______________ his best in his job. He never ______________ anything for granted. He regularly ______________ the night shift to ______________ his colleagues a favor as they have families and he is single. Even though he is often tired, he ______________ his job his all. Last night a woman arrived in the hospital. Her husband had been ______________ her a ride to the hospital when she went into labor. They decided not to ______________ a risk and called an ambulance. She had ______________ birth in the ambulance. The paramedics had ______________ a great job. Both mother and baby are ______________ fine.

Exercise 7

What does a patient ***do***, ***give*** and ***take***?

____

____

____

____

____

Exercise 8

What does a doctor ***do***, ***give*** and ***take***?

Exercise 9

Write medical sentences using ***do, give*** and ***take***.

Exercise 10

1. Write your own question and answer using ***take***.

2. Write your own question and answer using ***give***.

3. Write your own question and answer using ***do***.

Don't bring me down.

Bring

Examples

Bring about
The cancer was brought about by smoking.
Bring out
I'm allergic to apples, they bring me out in a rash.
Bring up
I was brought up by my grandmother.
Bring back
I'm very tired, coffee will bring me back to life.
Bring to
Can you bring a sample to the clinic?

Bring down
We need to bring his fever down.
Bring along
Bring your daughter along to your next appointment.
Bring off
The surgeon brought off the difficult operation.
Bring home
You can bring your wife home tomorrow.
Bring forward
The date of your operation has been brought forward.

Exercise 1

Make a list of other medical collocations of ***bring***.

___

___

___

___

___

___

___

___

___

Exercise 2

Match the phrasal verbs on the left with the correct definition on the right.

1. Bring up __I__	A. Take something to the place where you live
2. Bring up_____	B. To return something
3. Bring up_____	C. Depress
4. Bring down_____	D. Connect or join
5. Bring down_____	E. To raise a point
6. Bring change_____	F. To make something different
7. Bring back_____	G. Successful
8. Bring home_____	H. Cause to fall
9. Bring off_____	I. Raise a child
10. Bring together_____	J. Vomit

Exercise 3

Write the missing words in the blank spaces.

story / alcohol / son / condition / ~~lunch~~ / smelling salts / bag / something / you / pictures / memories / fainted / worst / textbook / senses / hysterical

1. I brought up my ____**lunch**____ yesterday. I think I had food poisoning.
2. Bring your _______________ back to see me if his _______________ doesn't improve.
3. Hearing his sad _______________ brought me down.
4. _______________ brings out the _______________ in me.
5. This medical English _______________ was brought out in 2020.
6. Nurse, please bring a _______________ of type A blood.
7. Mr Smith, thank you for coming to see me. There is _______________ I need to bring up with _______________.
8. Do these _______________ bring back any _______________?
9. When Sally _______________, we brought her to with _______________.
10. The lady was _______________, a gentle slap brought her to her _______________.

Exercise 4

Write sentences using ***bring*** and the words from exercises 2 and 3.

____

____

____

____

____

Exercise 5

Read the passage then answer the questions.

Firefighters bring it!

Local firefighters brought everything they had to bear when they attended the scene of a huge blaze at a fireworks factory last night. They brought three fire trucks each bringing three hoses to the blaze. The blaze was eventually brought under control after five hours. They successfully brought it off with teamwork and great skill. The structure of the building was badly damaged and will have to be brought safely down after an investigation has been completed. The safety procedures at the factory have been brought into question, the police have brought the manager of the factory in for questioning. The police have declined to comment on the case.

1. What did the firefighters bring to the fire?

<u>They brought three fire trucks.</u>

2. How long did it take for the blaze to be brought under control?

____

3. What will happen to the building?

____

4. Does the factory have good safety procedures?

____

5. Where is the manager of the factory?

____

Exercise 6

Put the sentences in the correct order and write ***bring*** in its correct form in the sentence.

1. patient to room examination _______________ the one.

Bring the patient to examination room one.

2. What meeting did you _______________ up in yesterday the?

____

3. Feeling back weak, really so _______________ him down earth to.

____

4. The disrepute relationship with hospital the doctor's patient the into.

____

5. The hives bar _______________ my peanut son chocolate out in.

____

6. I _______________ a second nice hot bowl of soup up to my wife in house our chicken bedroom on the floor of our.

____

7. The ambulance is being _______________as quickly as possible by heart.

____

8. Dr Smith thinking round eventually _______________Dr Jones to his way of.

____

9. Please, _______________your insurance health to your next appointment documents.

____

10. He well up wasn't _______________.

____

Exercise 7

What must a patient ***bring*** when they have to stay overnight in hospital?

____

____

____

____

____

Exercise 8

What do these idioms mean?

1. Bring someone to heel

____

2. Bring somebody to their knees

____

Exercise 9

Write medical sentences using **bring**.

____

____

____

____

____

Exercise 10

Answer the questions.

1. If someone has fainted, how can you bring them around?

____

____

2. What would you like to bring up at your next meeting?

____

____

3. Who brought you up?

____

____

4. When was the last time you brought up your food?

____

____

5. What do you always bring with you to work?

____

____

I've come to a conclusion.

Come

Examples

Come home

The doctor told me that I could come home.

Come back

Please, come back Mrs Smith. You are very ill.

Come down with

I think I'm coming down with something.

Come up with

We need to come up with some ideas.

Come to an end

Your course of antibiotics will come to an end tomorrow.

Come to a conclusion

I've come to a conclusion about what to do.

Come prepared

Come prepared with a pen and paper.

Come first

Patients always come first.

Come in

May I come in?

Come to a stop

The car came to a stop and didn't hit me.

Exercise 1

Make a list of other medical collocations of ***come***.

___

___

___

___

___

___

___

___

___

Exercise 2

Unscramble the highlighted words, then write the full sentence.

back / prepared / under / clean / ~~**time**~~ / time / hospital / money / realization / over

1. Please come on tmie _______________to your next appointment Mrs Smith.
Please, come on **time** to your next appointment Mrs Smith.

2. Come directly to **hpistoal** as soon as you can.

____

3. You need to tell me the truth. You have to come **aclne** about your use of illegal drugs.

____

4. Come **ppadrere** with enough clothes to stay in hospital for at least two weeks.

____

5. After his grandfather died, Bob came into a lot of **eymon**.

____

6. He seemed to come **cabk** to life after the doctor injected him with epinephrine.

____

7. The group of soldiers came **duner** attack by the enemy.

____

8. I have come to the **tionizareal** that I need therapy.

____

9. Can you come **roev**? I need some help.

____

10. Don't worry he'll be here. The doctor always comes on **emti**.

____

Exercise 3

Write the correct words in the blank spaces.

~~come over~~ / comes first / came into some money / come Tuesday / came off worst / came to blows
come up with / came through / come to mention it / coming to terms

1. **Come over** to the hospital as soon as you can.
2. He helped me a lot, he really ____________________ for me.
3. Since I ____________________, I can afford private health insurance.
4. I'm having trouble ____________________ with my wife's death.
5. The blue car ____________________ in the accident.
6. ____________________ the operation will be all finished and you will be back at home.
7. The two drunk men ____________________ and both ended up in hospital.
8. We need to ____________________ some new ideas about how to better manage this hospital.
9. ____________________, I did eat some strange food while I was on vacation.
10. The well-being of our patients always ____________________.

Exercise 4

Match the idioms and phrases on the left with the correct definition on the right.

1. come alive __**B**__
2. come to a head _____
3. come clean _____
4. come a cropper _____
5. come at a price _____
6. come to blows _____
7. come in handy _____
8. one's number comes up _____
9. Come again? _____
10. come across _____

A. to have a misfortune
B. reanimate
C. to admit to a wrongdoing
D. to reach a critical stage when action must be taken
E. to get into a fight
F. to have a negative consequence
G. to be useful
H. to find
I. to be lucky or unlucky
J. Can you say that again?

Exercise 5

Write medical English sentences using the idioms and phrases from exercise 4.

1. ______________________________
2. ______________________________
3. ______________________________
4. ______________________________
5. ______________________________
6. ______________________________

Exercise 6

Correct the mistakes.

1. We need to come to an ~~**argument**~~ about his treatment.

We need to come to an **agreement** about his treatment.

2. He has a terminal illness. His life will come to an finish within six months.

____

3. The new uniforms for the staff come down white.

____

4. The medical student came to a plan, she decided to specialize in dermatology.

____

5. I need to come dirty about something.

____

6. Can I come down tonight? I need your help to study for the physiology exam.

____

7. The victim finally came into money when the sun started to rise.

____

8. This first-aid kit comes missing with adhesive bandages, antiseptic wipes and a first-aid manual.

____

9. I'll come left back with your medication.

____

10. The firefighter came to my home when I was trapped in a burning building.

____

Exercise 7

Complete the conversations. There might be more than one correct answer.

Conversation 1

A. Good morning Mrs Jones. Thank you for ______________.

B. Hello doctor. Why did you want to see me?

A. Your test results have ______________.

B. And?

A. It's not good news I'm afraid.

B. Oh well. Luckily, I ______________mentally ______________for bad news.

A. There are some treatment options. Let's talk about them and ______________to a ______________.

Conversation 2

A. I went to see the doctor this morning. He gave me bad news about my condition.

B. I see.

A. He told me to discuss it with you and ______________to an ______________together. Now that my life is ______________to an ______________, I've decided not to have any further treatment.

B. Oh.

A. I've ______________to the ______________that I'd like to die at home with my family rather than in a hospital.

B. I don't think I can ______________to ______________with that decision. Can't we ______________to a ______________?

A. No, sorry. Please respect my decision.

Exercise 8

Write sentences with similar meanings.

1. Please, come in.

Enter!

2. The soldiers came under attack.

____

3. I couldn't come up with any good ideas about how to lose weight.

____

4. The monster in the horror movie came back to life.

____

5. I can't come to terms with your decision.

____

Exercise 9

Write medical sentences using ***come***.

Exercise 10

Answer the questions.

1. Do you need to come to a decision?

2. Do you need to come clean about anything?

3. What would you like to come to an end?

4. Who or what comes first in your life?

5. Have you ever come a cropper?

I got better.

Get

Examples

Get a disease

I've got a cold.

Get permission

I got permission to go home.

Get over an illness

She got over the flu last week.

Get an object

I'll get the chart for you doctor.

Get upset

She is going to get upset when we tell her.

Get old

My father is getting older.

Get by

I can't get by on my salary.

Get down

Staying in hospital for so long is getting me down.

Get hot

The patient is getting hotter.

Get cold

It will get cold tomorrow.

Exercise 1

Make a list of other medical collocations of ***get***.

Exercise 2

Unscramble the words then write the words in the blank spaces.

~~appointment~~ / house / water / medicine / morning / uncle / permission / upset / winter / chair

1. Have you got an atmoineppnt **appointment**?
2. Don't get so ptuse _____________, it's only a small mistake.
3. Can you get me a glass of aterw _____________, please?
4. I couldn't get out of bed this ngmnior _____________.
5. I've got the flu, please get me some iicmedne _____________.
6. You can't come in. You need to get iserpmonsi _____________.
7. My lnuce _____________ is getting old and he has no one to look after him.
8. Get out of the car and go inside the shoue _____________.
9. Wnitre _____________ is coming, it's getting colder.
10. I'll get you a hciar _____________, stand here for a moment.

Exercise 3

Match the beginning of the sentences on the left with the correct ending on the right.

1.Get back __**C**__	A. a cup of coffee.
2. I don't understand, _____	B. prescription filled.
3. Please, get me _____	C. from the edge.
4. I only got five _____	D. opinion.
5. Put antiseptic cream on it to _____	E. get to the point.
6. My back is _____	F. getting stiff.
7. I want to get a second _____	G. hours of sleep.
8. I need to get my _____	H. stop it from getting infected.
9. I got a _____	I. call from my doctor.
10. I got fired for _____	J. stealing medicine.

Exercise 4

Write the words using the clues to help you.

1. You need to get this before you can drive a car. You need a **driving licence**.
2. It takes me longer to do things these days. I must be getting _ _ _.
3. My wound is dirty, it got _ _ _ _ _ _ _ _ _ _ _ _.
4. I danced. I got _ _ _ _ _.
5. She is crying. She got _ _ _ _ _
6. I need a cup of coffee. I'm getting _ _ _ _ _ _.
7. I need to go to the pharmacy to get my _.
8. Leave my house, now! Get _ _ _!
9. Turn on the heater. I'm getting _ _ _ _ _.
10. I haven't gotten the flu so far this year. I haven't gotten _ _ _ _ _.

Exercise 5

Finish the sentences using your own ideas. Try to write medical examples.

1. I got ____.
2. I didn't get ____.
3. I need to get ____.
4. I've never gotten ____.
5. I want to get ____.
6. She is getting ____.
7. It hasn't got any ____.
8. They like to get____.
9. Can you get ____?
10. I don't have time to get ____.

Exercise 6

Cross out the incorrect answer.

1. I don't feel well. I think I've got _______________.

~~A. warm~~ B. a cold C. a fever D. a stomachache

2. I'm upset I got ______________ marks in my medical exam.

A. bad B. top C. poor D. terrible

3. I'm out of shape so I get ______________ when I run for more than 1km.

A. out of breath B. tired C. out of air D. exhausted

4. I got ______________ last Saturday night and threw up.

A. blind drunk B. deaf drunk C. dead drunk D. roaring drunk

5. I get ______________ before I take a shower.

A. naked B. undressed C. disrobed D. clothed

6. You need to get your parent's ______________ before you can have surgery. You are still underage.

A. consent B. authorization C. permission D. permit

Exercise 7

Put the telephone conversation into the correct order.

__1__A. I will come to visit you tomorrow. Is there anything you need?

_____A. I don't think that's a good idea. I don't want to get in trouble. Did you get permission from your doctor?

_____A. Is there anything else? It's getting dark, I want to get your things then get home before it gets too late.

_____A. Sure. What would you like?

_____A. Okay. Snacks got it.

_____B. No, that's all thank you. You should get off.

_____B. Could you also get me a small bottle of whisky?

_____B. Yes, could you get me a few things from the supermarket?

_____B. Please, get me some snacks.

_____B. I will ask her, but I don't think she will let me get drunk while I'm in hospital.

Exercise 8

Which of the following words collocate with ***get***? Underline the correct answers.

a nap / **a headache** / a sleep / happy / a class / a cold / hurt / people / annoyed / frightened / sick
a decision / fit / into trouble / lessons / pregnant / deaf / a shock / crazy / exercise

Exercise 9

Write medical sentences using ***get***.

Exercise 10

Answer the questions.

1. What time do you usually get up?

2. When was the last time you got sick?

3. What gets you down?

4. Who do you get along with?

5. What would you like to get into?

Do you want me to come and get it? Will you bring it?

Review

Exercise 1

Write the words in the correct space in the table. Some words might have more than one correct answer.

~~life~~ / to terms with / early / up / off / back / to mind / down / change / to a decision / closer / to an end angry / divorced / married / a cold / sick / together / lost / last / out / over / to a head / alive / forth / in

Bring	Come	Get
life		

Exercise 2

Write the correct form of ***bring***, ***come*** or ***get*** in the blank spaces.

1. The doctors <u>**came**</u> to an agreement about which medication to prescribe to the patient.
2. The professor always _______________ out the best in his medical students.
3. The procedure _______________ bad press, but it is effective.
4. My internship at this hospital is _______________ to an end.
5. Can you _______________ closer? My eyes aren't what they used to be.
6. I'm afraid I've _______________ bad news about your husband.
7. There is no need to _______________ angry. Please, calm down.
8. When you _______________ the chance, please make an appointment to see me.

Exercise 3

Match the beginning of the sentences on the left with the correct ending on the right.

1. My wife brought up her __K__
2. The doctor told me that _____
3. I was worried that _____
4. I brought _____
5. After hearing the news, _____
6. I asked when she might have _____
7. I had gotten sent _____
8. I got shocked _____
9. I must come _____
10. We might _____
11. I might bring it up _____
12. I'm not sure what I will do _____

A. as if it was my own.
B. she had gotten pregnant.
C. her to hospital.
D. she had gotten sick.
E. an uneasy feeling came over me.
F. to prison at that time.
G. by his answer.
H. gotten into this condition.
I. get divorced.
J. when the baby comes.
K. breakfast this morning.
L. to a decision.

Exercise 4

Write down the sentences from exercise 3 to make a story.

____
____
____
____
____
____
____

Exercise 5

Finish the sentences with your own ideas. Try to use medical examples.

1. Would you like to come ____?
2. Please, bring ____.
3. Can you get me some ____?
4. I've got ____.
5. I would like to get ____.
6. I wouldn't like to get____.

Exercise 6

Correct the mistake in the sentences. ***Bring***, ***come*** and ***get*** have been used incorrectly.

1. I ~~got~~ **brought** some medical students with me to observe, is that okay?
2. Can you bring a little closer? I need to examine you.
3. When did you brought this? It looks infected.
4. How did you got this? It looks painful.
5. When I come, no one was here, so I went to a different clinic.
6. I need you to brought some sedatives for this patient as soon as possible.

Exercise 7

What do these idioms mean?

1. Bring up-to-date

____

2. Bring to one's senses

____

3. Come back to haunt one

____

Exercise 8

Write questions to match the answers.

1.
Q. What time did you get here?
A. I got here at twelve o'clock. You were sleeping when I came.
2.
Q. ____?
A. Sure. Would you like milk and sugar?
3.
Q. ____?
A. I have a sore throat and a fever.

Exercise 9

Write medical sentences using ***bring***, ***come*** and ***get***.

Exercise 10

1. Write your own question and answer using ***bring***.

2. Write your own question and answer using ***come***.

3. Write your own question and answer using ***get***.

I’m feeling better.

Feel

Examples

Feel tired

I feel really tired. I’m going to bed.

Feel sick

I feel sick. I shouldn’t have eaten that.

Feel unwell

Bob felt unwell, so he went home.

Feel like

I feel like I’m going to throw up.

Feel nauseous

Pregnant women sometimes feel nauseous.

Feel about

How do you feel about leaving the hospital today?

Feel comfortable/uncomfortable

The cast feels uncomfortable.

Feel hot/cold

I feel too hot.

Feel hungry/thirsty

I don’t feel hungry. I’m full.

Feel uneasy

I’m feeling a little uneasy about my operation.

Exercise 1

Make a list of other medical collocations of ***feel***.

Exercise 2

Unscramble the words.

1. Feel nrvoeus

Feel **nervous**.

2. Feel uptse

Feel _______________

3. Feel nnaedoy

Feel _______________

4. Feel ptyi

Feel _______________

5. No hdra feelings

Feel _______________

6. Srtgon feelings

Feel _______________

7. Feel dpeely

Feel _______________

8. Feel like a eerb

Feel _______________

9. Feel izdyz

Feel _______________

10. Feel kaoy

Feel _______________

Exercise 3

Write the correct form of ***feel*** in the blank spaces.

1. The patient's skin **felt** cold.
2. The patient is _______________ terrible because of the pain.
3. He has been _______________ like death for a long time.
4. She _______________ someone touch her arm.
5. I _______________ a flash of pain when the man punched me in the face.
6. I can't _______________ a pulse.
7. Who is _______________ unwell?
8. Can you _______________this?
9. You've hurt his _______________.
10. I'm _______________ good.

Exercise 4

Circle the five positive emotion words and underline the five negative emotion words.

pessimistic	inferior	confident	optimistic	jealousy
joy	content	proud	hatred	anxious

Exercise 5

Write sentences using ***feel*** and the words from exercise 4.

1. I'm feeling confident about my exam results.
3. ______________________________
4. ______________________________
5. ______________________________
6. ______________________________
7. ______________________________
8. ______________________________
9. ______________________________
10. ______________________________

Exercise 6

Search the Internet or check a thesaurus to find ten more emotions and write sentences using ***feel***.

1. I've been feeling **lonely** since my wife left me.
2. ______________________________
3. ______________________________
4. ______________________________
5. ______________________________
6. ______________________________
7. ______________________________
8. ______________________________
9. ______________________________
10. ______________________________

Exercise 7

Read the letters between a therapist and a patient then answer the questions.

Dear Dr Jones,
Recently I've been feeling blue. I went out drinking to try and drown my sorrows, I only had a couple of beers, but I woke up feeling like death. I'm really feeling my age even though I'm only 39. My wife left me about a month ago she said that she hadn't been feeling like herself while she was married to me. I bumped into her the other day and she has a new boyfriend. She told me she feels like a new woman. That made me feel quite small. I feel lost, please help me.
Kind regards,
Jim.

Dear Jim,
I understand how you feel. Many people feel this way. Alcohol isn't the answer. You need to stop feeling sorry for yourself. I know you feel hard done by, but you need to need to pick yourself up and meet someone new. Try getting some exercise, take up a new hobby or go on a date. A little exercise can make you feel like a million dollars.
Feel free to contact me anytime.
Take care,
Dr Jones.

1. How does Jim feel?

____

2. Why did Jim's wife leave him?

____

3. How does Jim's wife feel now?

____

4. What shouldn't Jim do?

____

5. What advice does the therapist give?

____

____

____

6. When can Jim contact the therapist?

____

Exercise 8

Write a letter to a therapist. Tell the therapist about your emotional problems.

Exercise 9

Write medical sentences using ***feel***.

Exercise 10

Answer the questions.

1. How are you feeling right now?

2. What do you do if a patient is feeling bored?

3. What makes you feel blue?

4. What makes you feel angry?

5. What makes you feel terrified?

I have a good feeling.

Have

Examples

Have a disease
Her grandfather has cancer.

Have a cold
Do you have a cold?

Have health insurance
The patient doesn't have health insurance.

Have a problem
Bob has a lot of problems.

Have sympathy
I don't have any sympathy for him.

Have a medical condition
My son has asthma.

Have the flu
I can't come to work today. I have the flu.

Have a wound/injury
I can't go skiing tomorrow. I have a broken leg.

Have an attack
Help. My husband is having a heart attack.

Have an appointment
You don't have an appointment today.

Exercise 1

Make a list of other medical collocations of ***have***.

____

____

____

____

____

____

____

____

____

Exercise 2

Match the synonyms.

1. have a break __**B**__
2. have a row _____
3. have a bite _____
4. have problems _____
5. have a reservation _____
6. have a relationship _____
7. have a test _____
8. have a party _____
9. have an upset stomach _____
10. have a rash _____

A. have an exam
B. have a rest
C. have an argument
D. have issues
E. have something to eat
F. have a boyfriend or girlfriend
G. have an appointment
H. have spots
I. have a get together
J. have a stomachache

Exercise 3

Complete the sentences. There might be more than one correct answer.

1. I've been throwing up and I have terrible diarrhea. I must have food **poisoning**.
2. My wife is pregnant. We are going to have a _______________.
3. When would you like to have your next _______________?
4. My mother is 80 years old, she can't remember things. She has _______________.
5. I'm dirty and smelly, I need to have a _______________.
6. We need to have a serious talk. Let's have a _______________.
7. At least try it. You need to have a _______________.
8. I'm feeling a little sleepy. I'm going to have a _______________.
9. Please, help me. I'm having a little _______________.
10. Please send an ambulance, my husband has had an _______________.

Exercise 4

Write the correct form of ***have*** in the blank spaces.

1. I **had** a cold last week. I **had** to take some medicine.
2. James is exhausted he needs to ______________a rest.
3. She can't afford to take a taxi to the hospital. She doesn't ______________any money.
4. My grandmother ______________Alzheimer's disease. She gets confused easily. I think she will ______________to move into a nursing home.
5. I've been ______________trouble sleeping recently. Last night I ______________a nightmare about zombies.
6. Do you ______________an appointment? We are ______________ problems with our PC so I can't check the schedule.
7. What ______________have you eaten today? I ______________a sandwich.
8. My wife ______________a baby last week, but I ______________met him yet.
9. He ______________a lot of work to do, but he doesn't ______________enough time.
10. ______________you seen my husband? He was taken to hospital this morning. I think he might ______________ ______________ a heart attack. He ______________brown hair and green eyes.

Exercise 5

Read the conversation then answer the questions.

A: Hi James, please sit down on the sofa.
B: Thanks.
A: Tell me what's troubling you today?
B: I've been having problems with my wife.
A: What kind of problems?
B: She has been yelling at me a lot recently.
A: Why do you think that might be?
B: I'm not sure. Maybe she has a lot of stress and hasn't been sleeping well. Maybe it's something that I have or have not done. To be honest I have no idea.
A: How have you been feeling?
B: A little lonely. I cope by having a few drinks every night.
A: Have you had a drink today?
B: I haven't had anything.
A: You can tell me the truth. This conversation is confidential.
B: Okay, yes. I've been drinking all day.
A: I thought so. You have bad breath, you also seemed to stumble when you arrived. I think you might have a drinking problem.
B: Oh.
A: If you have time, I think you should join my counselling group for alcoholics. You can have a friendly chat with people who have the same kind of problems.
B: I don't have time to go to group therapy, I'm too busy.
A: Hmm, I really think you should try to cut down on your drinking. Have a soft drink instead sometimes.

1. Why did James visit the counsellor?
He has been having problems with his wife.
2. What has James' wife been doing that upset James?

____

3. How has James been feeling?

____

4. How is James' hygiene?

____

5. What is James' problem?

____

6. What should James do?

____

7. Can James follow the counsellor's advice?

____

Exercise 6

Finish the sentences with your own ideas.

1. I had an argument ______________________________.
2. You need to have ______________________________.
3. Why don't you have a go ______________________________.
4. I have never ______________________________.

Exercise 7

Circle the correct words to complete the sentences.

1. My cat had **kittens / puppies / cubs** yesterday. We are having a little **easy / trouble / problems** looking after them.
2. I have put on **weight / fat / heavy** recently. I have to **start / continue / stop** eating junk food.
3. I have twelve patients to look after in my ward. I'm going to have a **crowded / busy / easy** day tomorrow.
4. Bob has to go to **hospital / home / prison** for three years, before now he had never been in **trouble / problems / difficulty** with the law.
5. The president of the company had a major heart **assault / stroke / attack**. He has to have heart **surgery / operation / procedure**.

Exercise 8

What do these idioms mean?

1. have cold feet

2. have a big head

Exercise 9

Write medical sentences using ***have***.

Exercise 10

Answer the questions.

1. What do you do if you have a headache?

2. Have you been sick recently?

3. Do you have any regrets?

4. How have you been?

5. What responsibilities do you have at work?

You made it.

Make

Examples

Make an appointment

I would like to make an appointment.

Make a mess

Someone has made a mess in the toilet.

Make a complaint

I would like to make a complaint.

Make a difference

It won't make any difference.

Make plans

Don't make any plans.

Make up

We had an argument, but we have made up now.

Make a call

Can I make a call to my wife?

Make a decision

You have a decision to make.

Make progress

The patient has been making good progress.

Make sure

We need to make sure it isn't cancer.

Exercise 1

Make a list of other medical collocations of ***make***.

____

____

____

____

____

____

____

____

____

Exercise 2

Choose A, B or C.

1. I need to do some tests to make **A**.

~~A. sure~~ B. of course C. correct

2. Your next ______________ is on May 9th.

A. meeting B. appointment C. date

3. What would you like me to make for your ______________?

A. lunch B. drink C. food

4. Have you made any ______________with your report?

A. support B. progress C. help

5. Stop arguing! You need to make ______________.

A. down B. up C. below

6. Check again to make sure ______________.

A. yes B. sure C. yeah

7. You've made a terrible ______________. Clean it up!

A. dirty B. mess C. messy

8. A positive attitude makes a big ______________.

A. difference B. different C. difficult

9. I'm sorry, but your husband didn't make ______________.

A. that B. it C. this

10. Mrs Jones isn't happy. She wants to make a ______________.

A. complaining B. claim C. complaint

Exercise 3

Match the questions with the answers. There might be more than one correct answer.

1. Can you make me a sandwich? **D H**
2. Who made the complaint? _____
3. Did you make up with your boyfriend? _____
4. Can you make a report for me? _____
5. Do I need therapy? _____
6. Where was this medicine made? _____
7. Who did you make love to? _____
8. Why are you wearing make-up? _____
9. When is your next appointment? _____
10. Why do you look made up? _____

A. I proposed to my girlfriend. She said yes.
B. I'm an actor in a movie.
C. I made it for next Tuesday.
D. Sure.
E. Yes, you do. It will make a big difference.
F. In Japan.
G. To my wife, who else?
H. Of course.
I. Mrs. Green did.
J. No, I'm waiting for him to apologize first.

Exercise 4

Fill in the blank space. Some words are extra. Some words can be used more than once.

coffee / mess / ~~better~~ / sick / friends / up / love/ appointment / take / well / sure / baby / over / sad / tired
upset / angry / happy / life / mistake / healthy / meeting / lunch / report / difference / progress

1.
A. Can you make me **better** doctor?
B. I'll do my best.
2.
A. This medicine makes me _______________. What should I do?
B. Don't worry we will put you on different medication.
3.
A. Who made a _______________ in the toilet? It's very dirty.
B. I think it was Mr Smith in room 201.
4.
A. What makes you _______________ Mrs Jones?
B. Nothing does, these days.
5.
A. When would you like to make your next _______________?
B. Friday morning at nine, please.
6.
A. My daughter won't take her medicine. How can I make her _______________ it?
B. Try this medicine for kids. It tastes a little nicer.
7.
A. I'm miserable every day. How can I make my _______________ better?
B. Try making a little time for yourself every day.
8.
A. Will this medicine make me _______________ again, doctor?
B. Let's wait and see.
9.
A. The doctor made a _______________. He amputated the wrong leg.
B. Oh, dear!
10.
A. Bob and his wife are trying to make a _______________.
B. Really? Bob always said he never wanted kids.

Exercise 5

Fill in the blank space with a phrase from answer choices **A** to **O**. Some phrases are extra.

A. made him very angry
B. make some changes
C. make all of your payments
D. is being made
E. must refrain
F. make a note
G. make an exception
H. make an effort
I. made a good point
J. make a suggestion
K. make the bed
L. make enough money
M. makes sense
N. made a sound
~~**O. made a mistake**~~

1. Your appointment is on Thursday not Tuesday. I think you have **O**.
2. I understand that you are hungry. Your lunch _______________ as we speak.
3. I'm afraid you don't have health insurance. Did you _______________?
4. Be careful with that patient, someone has _______________.
5. I know it's difficult, but physical therapy is important to help you get better. Please, _______________.
6. Please tell me your contact details, I need to _______________ of them for our records.
7. Usually we can't do that, but for you I will _______________.
8. Until your injury heals, you _______________ from making love to your wife.
9. I don't have private health insurance. I don't _______________ to pay for it.
10. Can I _______________? Why don't you go home and rest?

Exercise 6

Make can be used to talk about feelings and emotions. Answer the questions.

What makes you happy?

____

____

____

What makes you sad?

____

____

____

What makes you angry?

____

____

____

Exercise 7

Read the passage then answer the questions.

Little Bobby was very young when he died. He had an accident which made him cry. He was hit by a car and seriously injured. The car caused lots of cuts all over his body which made him bleed terribly. His parents didn't make much money so they couldn't pay for a taxi to take him to hospital. They had to make their own way there. They hadn't been making payments on their health insurance, so the hospital refused to treat Bobby. However, a kind nurse made a call to her rich friend who agreed to help. There weren't enough beds in the hospital, but somehow, they made room. Everyone made the best of a bad situation. Unfortunately, Bobby didn't make it.

1. Why did Bobby cry?

____

____

____

2. Why couldn't the parents pay for a taxi or health insurance?

____

____

____

3. How did they get to the hospital?

____

____

____

4. Who made an effort to help?

____

____

____

5. Was Bobby okay in the end?

____

____

____

Exercise 8

Make up your own medical story.

____

____

____

____

____

____

____

Exercise 9

Write medical sentences using ***make***.

Exercise 10

Answer the questions.

1. If you make someone upset, how can you make it up to them?

2. Your friend is depressed. How can you make them happy?

3. What can you make well?

4. You have a cold. What can you do to make yourself better?

5. How do you make a traditional remedy in your country?

How have you been feeling? Can I make something for you?

Review

Exercise 1

Complete the word search.

D	I	F	F	E	R	E	N	C	E	P	L	A	N	S
I	X	T	A	I	I	L	Q	N	H	F	H	G	F	Y
S	N	K	Q	G	U	L	L	A	R	J	U	I	R	M
E	P	L	M	F	G	W	O	U	N	D	G	R	W	P
A	I	O	A	D	D	S	J	S	S	Q	H	A	D	A
S	I	C	K	S	R	E	F	E	F	G	S	F	B	T
E	R	O	E	W	W	T	E	O	E	J	P	F	I	H
T	S	M	X	N	S	I	X	U	V	S	R	E	U	Y
H	F	P	R	O	G	R	E	S	S	D	O	S	F	I
J	H	L	T	B	J	E	B	J	S	A	B	O	U	T
I	H	A	V	E	D	D	O	W	N	T	L	T	E	H
W	F	I	E	D	S	H	C	K	E	I	E	I	J	O
S	E	N	W	A	P	P	O	I	N	T	M	E	N	T
B	E	T	T	E	R	J	L	L	K	P	E	L	Z	L
B	L	P	K	S	Y	W	D	E	L	O	D	W	X	J

~~feel~~ / make / have / better / tired / sick / nauseous / wound / appointment / disease / complaint
difference / progress / problem / sympathy / plans / hot / cold / down / about

Exercise 2

Unscramble the words. Then write ***feel***, ***have*** or ***make***.

1. odgo ______**feel**______ ______**good**______
2. coesnfsoni ____________ _ _ _ _ _ _ _ _ _ _
3. kebaacch ____________ _ _ _ _ _ _ _ _
4. rsroy ____________ _ _ _ _ _
5. dovsceryi ____________ _ _ _ _ _ _ _ _ _
6. nnfuy ____________ _ _ _ _ _
7. rncnedcoe ____________ _ _ _ _ _ _ _ _ _
8. tserko ____________ _ _ _ _ _ _
9. cueexs ____________ _ _ _ _ _ _
10. pexontcei ____________ _ _ _ _ _ _ _ _ _

Exercise 3

Write sentences using the words from exercise 2.

1. I'm feeling good for the first time in a long while.
2. ____
3. ____
4. ____
5. ____
6. ____
7. ____
8. ____
9. ____
10. ____

Exercise 8

Write a conversation between a doctor and a patient using ***feel***, ***have*** and ***make***.

D.____

P. ____

D.____

P. ____

D.____

P. ____

Exercise 9

Write medical sentences using ***feel, have*** and ***make***.

Exercise 10

1. Write your own question and answer using ***feel***.

2. Write your own question and answer using ***have***.

3. Write your own question and answer using ***make***.

Answers

UNIT 1 TAKE

P.6

Exercise 2

1. I'm going to take **you** to the operating room.
2. You look tired. You should take a **break**.
3. Take two **tablets** three times a day after meals.
4. He hasn't taken a **bath** for three months. He is very dirty!
5. I'm not going to take **responsibility** for that. It's not my fault.
6. I took a **taxi** to the hospital.
7. Bob hasn't taken a **shower** for two weeks. He is quite smelly.
8. I gave up my job to take **care** of my elderly mother.
9. Nurse, please take Mr. Johnson's **temperature**.
10. I'm afraid he has been taking illegal **drugs**.

P.6

Exercise 3

1.F 2.I 3.A 4.D 5.E 6.C 7.H 8.B 9.G 10.J

P.7

Exercise 4

A: Good morning Mrs Jones. Please take a **seat**.

B: Thanks.

A: What seems to be the trouble?

B: I've been very tired recently. I just can't seem to sleep.

A: Have you been taking **anything** to help you sleep?

B: Yes, I've been taking over the counter herbal **medication**, but it hasn't been working.

A: Have you had any stress in your life recently?

B: Yes, both at home and at work. I think my husband has been taking me **for granted**. I can't do everything.

A: I see. You sound very busy. Maybe your trouble sleeping is down to stress. Can you take a short **vacation**, just by yourself?

B: No way, I've got too much to do?

A: Okay, well let me give you a prescription for some sleeping pills. Take it to the **pharmacy**. Only take a maximum of **one pill a day**. Do not take more than that. Stop taking **herbal** medication. Don't take both at the same time.

B: I understand.

A: If possible, take some **time** for yourself every day. Maybe take up **yoga**.

B: Thank you doctor.

A: You're welcome. Take **care**.

P.7

Exercise 5

1. medicine	a pill	a tablet	~~antiseptic cream~~
2. your time	a break	~~sleep~~	a nap
3. ~~through~~	down	up	out
4. a day off	a holiday	time off	~~free time~~
5. ~~a phone~~	a call	a message	advice
6. a shower	~~a toilet~~	a bath	a wet tissue
7. ~~foot~~	a bus	an ambulance	a taxi
8. care	after	~~a see~~	advantage
9. off	on	~~at~~	in
10. a blood test	an x-ray	~~a heart review~~	an eye exam

P.8

Exercise 6

1. Doctor: Hello, please take a seat.
2. Patient: Thank you.
3. Doctor: What seems to be the trouble?
4. Patient: I've had a headache for the past five days.
5. Doctor: Have you taken anything for it?
6. Patient: I've been taking aspirin, but it hasn't worked.
7. Doctor: Here is a prescription for some stronger pain killers. Only take two every four hours. These pills can take about ten minutes to take effect.
8. Patient: Thank you, doctor.
9. Doctor: Take my advice and take a rest.
10. Patient: I will. Thanks again.

P.8

Exercise 7

1. Why is the man in hospital?
He had taken an overdose of drugs.
2. What kind of drugs had he taken?
He had taken heroin.
3. What did the doctors take from the patient?
They took some blood.
4. How did he escape from prison?
He assaulted a guard and took his uniform and keys.
5. Why was the man in prison?
He is a conman who took advantage of the elderly and took their money.

P.9

Exercise 8

1. The person can't cope with the current situation.
2. He gets angry when he is made fun of or tricked.

P.9

Exercise 10

Example answers.

1. What do you always take on vacation?

I always take wet tissues.

2. Why might a doctor need to take blood from a patient?

To evaluate how well some organs are working.

3. Do you take supplements?

Yes, I do. I take multivitamins every day.

4. Who do you take after?

I take after my father. We are both workaholics.

5. What did you take from this lesson?

I learned how to use take in medical English.

UNIT 2 GIVE

P.11

Exercise 2

												P		
H	O	P	E						C			E		
	P								H			R		C
	I								O			M		O
	N				D	A	D	V	I	C	E	I		L
	I				I				C			S		D
	O	B			S				E			S		
	N	I			E							I		
		R			A							O		
		T			S							N	H	
		H			E								A	
							M	E	D	I	C	I	N	E
													D	
P	R	I	O	R	I	T	Y	E	X	A	M	P	L	E

P.11

Exercise 3

1. time 2. choice 3. lecture 4. ring 5. permission 6. thought 7. impression 8. answer 9. evidence 10. hug

P.12

Exercise 4

Example answers

1. I'm sorry, I can't give you any more of my time. The hospital is very busy today.
2. Can you give me another choice? I don't want to have surgery.
3. I have to give a lecture tomorrow at an international medical conference.
4. Don't forget to give your grandma a ring to remind her to take her medicine. Sometimes, she forgets.
5. I don't need you to give your permission. I can leave anytime I want. Can't I?
6. Have you given any thought to having the surgery?
7. The patient's father gave me the impression that he didn't care about his son's health.
8. Please, just give me a straight answer. What's wrong with me?
9. The forensic science technician gave evidence about the crime in court.
10. Give him a hug. He is depressed and lonely.

P.12

Exercise 5

1. Yesterday, I gave **blood** I'm type A. I donated about a pint.
2. My wife is due to give **birth** next month. I'm really nervous about becoming a father for the first time.
3. I will never forget the **advice** that my father gave me. He told me to work hard and believe in myself.
4. Eating too much ice cream, too quickly usually gives me a **stomachache**.
5. Can you give me some **aspirin**? I have a headache.
6. Those bags look heavy, can I give you a **hand**?
7. The exposed wire gave me an electric **shock**.
8. Would you mind giving me a **lift** to the hospital tomorrow?
9. Coffee gives me a **boost** of energy in the morning.
10. Please give me some more **time** I'm really busy.

P.13

Exercise 6

1. I gave my heavily pregnant wife a ride to the hospital hours before she gave birth.
2. Give priority to the patients with the most life-threatening injuries.
3. Don't give that man any more treatment. He is a hypochondriac, there isn't anything wrong with him.
4. Can you give me a hand lifting this patient? He is very heavy.
5. The patient's mother was so happy that she gave the doctor a kiss.
6. The lecture that Doctor Smith gave about parasites was interesting.
7. I don't give a damn about the risks! We must do the operation now.
8. I decided to stop smoking after the doctor gave me some advice.

P.13

Exercise 7

1. I can't give you any more morphine. You've already had the maximum dose.
2. I've tried very hard. I have nothing else to give.
3. The medical student didn't give himself enough time to finish his dissertation.
4. Would you like me to give you a hug?
5. I've given you the best advice I can.
6. I've decided to give up on my marriage and file for divorce.
7. Let's give our thoughts and prayers to Mrs Jones after the death of her son.

P.14

Exercise 8

1. I wasn't given a choice. The doctors wouldn't discharge me from hospital.
2. Can you give me some more morphine?
3. Would you like me to give you a hand with your bags?
4. We need you to give your permission to perform the operation on your husband.
5. Finding out the cause of the disease has been given the priority.
6. I'll give you a call later.
7. That loud music is giving me a headache.
8. Why don't you give a damn?
9. I have to give you some bad news about your condition.
10. I don't want to give you hope just yet.

P.15

Exercise 10

Example answers

1. What is the best piece of advice that you have ever been given?

My father told me to believe in myself.

2. Have you ever given blood?

I once gave blood during a blood drive at my university.

3. What advice can you give someone who wants to learn medical English?

Try to learn how to explain technical terms to native English speakers.

4. If you were given the choice, which would you choose; love, money or beauty?

I would choose money. Money doesn't bring happiness, but it helps to make life easier.

5. What gives you a headache?

I always get a bad headache after drinking white wine.

UNIT 3 DO

P.17

Exercise 2

1.A 2.B 3.A 4.C 5.A 6.C 7.C

P.18

Exercise 3

1. business 2. best 3. work 4. nothing 5. research 6. damage

P.18

Exercise 4

1. The medical student forgot to do his homework.
2. I need to do this medical report.
3. Smoking can do a lot of damage to your lungs.
4. The patient has wet the bed. We need to do the laundry
5. Can you do me a favour? I need some help with this patient.
6. I'm doing my best to stop drinking.

P.19

Exercise 5

Example answers

1. **Nutritionist**

A nutritionist creates specialized dietary plans.

2. **Surgeon**

A surgeon performs invasive medical procedures on patients.

3. **Physician**

Physicians examine patients, prescribe medications and perform diagnostic tests.

P.19 & 20

Exercise 6

Example answers

1. **What will Bob do at twenty past ten on Monday morning?**

He has an appointment with Julia Wilson.

2. **What will Sally do at half-past one on Sunday?**

She will have a meeting with Dr Simpson at West Clinic.

3. **What will Bob do on Friday?**

He has a breakfast meeting at seven o'clock in the morning. He has surgery hours from ten to midday and from two until six in the afternoon.

4. **What will Sally do on Sunday?**

She has three appointments in the morning. She has a meeting with Dr Simpson at half-past one in the afternoon. She has her regular staff meeting at half past four in the afternoon.

5. **What do you think about what Bob is doing on Monday evening, Thursday evening and Saturday evening?**

Bob is having dinner with three different women in the same week. He seems to be a womanizer. I don't think that is proper for someone in his position.

P.21

Exercise 7

Example answers

Hospital	
DO	**DON'T**
Wash your hands.	Disturb patients.
Be careful.	Use your cell phone/mobile phone.
Speak in an appropriate tone of voice.	Smoke.
Speak calmly.	Touch the medical equipment.
Keep noise to a minimum.	Take photos without permission.
Keep children with you at all times.	Bring animals inside unless they are assistance dogs.
Tell the truth.	Visit someone if you are sick.
Follow your doctor's instructions.	Lie.
Follow the hospital's rules.	Don't waste medical resources.

P.21

Exercise 8

1. Bend over backwards to do something

To work very hard to do something for someone.

2. Break one's back to do something

To put in a great effort to do something.

3. Do as I say, not as I do

Obey my instructions, even though I might not follow the instructions myself.

4. Do one's head in

To make someone feel angry or frustrated.

P.22

Exercise 10

Example answers

1. What do you do?

I'm a nurse.

2. What do you have a licence to do?

I have a licence to practice medicine.

3. What can you do well?

I can find a patient's vein very easily. I'm better than all of the other nurses in my clinic.

4. What can't you do very well?

I'm not very good at comforting a crying patient.

5. What does a nurse do?

A nurse cares for the sick and injured.

UNIT 4 REVIEW

P.23

Exercise 1

<table>
<tr><td></td><td></td><td></td><td>R</td><td></td><td>B</td><td></td><td></td><td></td><td></td><td></td><td></td><td></td><td></td><td></td></tr>
<tr><td>M</td><td>E</td><td>D</td><td>I</td><td>C</td><td>I</td><td>N</td><td>E</td><td></td><td></td><td></td><td>N</td><td>E</td><td>W</td><td>S</td></tr>
<tr><td></td><td>X</td><td></td><td>D</td><td></td><td>R</td><td></td><td></td><td></td><td></td><td></td><td>O</td><td></td><td></td><td></td></tr>
<tr><td>T</td><td>A</td><td>K</td><td>E</td><td></td><td>T</td><td></td><td></td><td>B</td><td>E</td><td>S</td><td>T</td><td></td><td></td><td></td></tr>
<tr><td></td><td>M</td><td></td><td></td><td></td><td>H</td><td>A</td><td>I</td><td>R</td><td></td><td></td><td>I</td><td></td><td></td><td>C</td></tr>
<tr><td></td><td>P</td><td></td><td></td><td></td><td></td><td></td><td></td><td>E</td><td></td><td></td><td>C</td><td>A</td><td>L</td><td>L</td></tr>
<tr><td></td><td>L</td><td>E</td><td>S</td><td>S</td><td>O</td><td>N</td><td></td><td>A</td><td></td><td></td><td>E</td><td></td><td></td><td>E</td></tr>
<tr><td></td><td>E</td><td></td><td>H</td><td></td><td></td><td></td><td></td><td>K</td><td></td><td></td><td></td><td></td><td></td><td>A</td></tr>
<tr><td>A</td><td></td><td>D</td><td>O</td><td></td><td></td><td>O</td><td>P</td><td>E</td><td>R</td><td>A</td><td>T</td><td>I</td><td>O</td><td>N</td></tr>
<tr><td>N</td><td></td><td></td><td>W</td><td></td><td>G</td><td></td><td></td><td></td><td></td><td></td><td></td><td></td><td></td><td>I</td></tr>
<tr><td>S</td><td></td><td>D</td><td>E</td><td>C</td><td>I</td><td>S</td><td>I</td><td>O</td><td>N</td><td></td><td></td><td></td><td></td><td>N</td></tr>
<tr><td>W</td><td></td><td></td><td>R</td><td></td><td>V</td><td></td><td></td><td></td><td></td><td></td><td></td><td>H</td><td>U</td><td>G</td></tr>
<tr><td>E</td><td></td><td></td><td></td><td></td><td>E</td><td></td><td></td><td></td><td></td><td></td><td></td><td>O</td><td></td><td></td></tr>
<tr><td>R</td><td></td><td></td><td></td><td></td><td></td><td></td><td></td><td></td><td></td><td></td><td></td><td>P</td><td></td><td></td></tr>
<tr><td></td><td></td><td>S</td><td>T</td><td>O</td><td>M</td><td>A</td><td>C</td><td>H</td><td>A</td><td>C</td><td>H</td><td>E</td><td></td><td></td></tr>
</table>

P.24

Exercise 2

Take	Give	Do
advice	advice	better
blood	answer	damage
break	birth	exercise
care	blood	harm
damage	choice	housework
exercise	credit	laundry
medicine	headache	maximum
notes	permission	paperwork
rest	priority	research
responsibility	responsibility	right thing
someone's temperature	stomachache	time
time	time	sums

P.24

Exercise 3

1.D 2.B 3.E 4.C 5.H 6.G 7.F 8.I 9.J 10.A

P.25

Exercise 6

Jim is a nurse. He always **does** his best in his job. He never **takes** anything for granted. He regularly **does** the night shift to **do** his colleagues a favor as they have families and he is single. Even though he is often tired, he **gives** his job his all. Last night a woman arrived in the hospital. Her husband had been **giving** her a ride to the hospital when she went into labor. They decided not to **take** a risk and called an ambulance. She had **given** birth in the ambulance. The paramedics had **done** a great job. Both mother and baby are **doing** fine.

UNIT 5 BRING

P.28

Exercise 2

1.I 2.J 3.E 4.C 5.H 6.F 7.B 8.A 9.G 10.D

P.28

Exercise 3

1. I brought up my **lunch** yesterday. I think I had food poisoning.
2. Bring your **son** back to see me if his **condition** doesn't improve.
3. Hearing his sad **story** brought me down.
4. **Alcohol** brings out the **worst** in me.
5. This medical English **textbook** was brought out in 2020.
6. Nurse, please bring a **bag** of type A blood.
7. Mr. Smith. Thank you for coming to see me. There is **something** I need to bring up with **you**.
8. Do these **pictures** bring back any **memories**?
9. When Sally **fainted**, we brought her to with **smelling salts**.
10. The lady was **hysterical**, a gentle slap brought her to her **senses**.

P.28

Exercise 5

1. What did the firefighters bring to the fire?

They brought three fire trucks.

2. How long did it take for the blaze to be brought under control?

It took five hours.

3. What will happen to the building?

It will be destroyed.

4. Does the factory have good safety procedures?

No, it doesn't.

5. Where is the manager of the factory?

The manager is at the police station.

P.30

Exercise 6

1. Bring the patient to examination room one.
2. What did you bring up in the meeting yesterday?
3. Feeling so weak, really brought him back down to earth.
4. The doctor's relationship with the patient brought the hospital into disrepute.
5. The peanut chocolate bar brought my son out in hives.
6. I brought a nice hot bowl of chicken soup up to my wife in our bedroom on the second floor of our house.
7. The heart is being brought as quickly as possible by ambulance.
8. Dr Smith eventually brought Dr Jones round to his way of thinking.
9. Please, bring your health insurance documents to your next appointment.
10. He wasn't brought up well.

P.31

Exercise 8

1. Bring someone to heel

To make someone obey.

2. Bring somebody to their knees

To defeat someone.

P.31

Exercise 10

Example answers

1. If someone has fainted, how can you bring them around?

I would use smelling salts to wake them up.

2. What would you like to bring up at your next meeting?

I would like to talk about patient care.

3. Who brought you up?

I was brought up by my parents in the UK.

4. When was the last time you brought up your food?

I ate bad sushi last month and then I threw up a few hours after lunch.

5. What do you always bring with you to work?

I always bring my diary and smartphone with me.

UNIT 6 COME

P.33

Exercise 2

1. Please come on **time** to your next appointment Mrs Smith.
2. Come directly to **hospital** as soon as you can.
3. You need to tell me the truth. You have to come **clean** about your use of illegal drugs.
4. Come **prepared** with enough clothes to stay in hospital for at least two weeks.
5. After his grandfather died, Bob came into a lot of **money**.
6. He seemed to come **back** to life after the doctor injected him with epinephrine.
7. The group of soldiers came **under** attack by the enemy.
8. I have come to the **realization** that I need therapy.
9. Can you come **over**? I need some help.
10. Don't worry he'll be here. The doctor always comes on **time**.

P.34

Exercise 3

1. **Come over** to the hospital as soon as you can.
2. He helped me a lot, he really **came through** for me.
3. Since I **came into some money**, I can afford private health insurance.
4. I'm having trouble **coming to terms** with my wife's death.
5. The blue car **came off** worst in the accident.
6. **Come Tuesday** the operation will be all finished and you will be back at home.
7. The two drunk men **came to blows** and both ended up in hospital.
8. We need to **come up with** some new ideas about how to better manage this hospital.
9. **Come to mention it**, I did eat some strange food while I was on vacation.
10. The well-being of our patients always **comes first**.

P.34

Exercise 4

1.B 2.D 3.C 4.A 5.F 6.E 7.G 8.I 9.J 10.H

P.35

Exercise 5

Example answers

1. It takes a couple of cups of coffee for me to come alive in the mornings.
2. Their relationship has finally come to a head.
3. What happened? You need to come clean about the cause of the accident.
4. Bob came a cropper when he was snowboarding.
5. His weight loss came at a price.
6. Bob and Ken came to blows over a woman.

P.35

Exercise 6

1. We need to come to an **agreement** about his treatment.
2. He has a terminal illness. His life will come to an **end** within six months.
3. The new uniforms for the staff come **in** white.
4. The medical student came to a **decision**, she decided to specialize in dermatology.
5. I need to come **clean** about something.
6. Can I come **over** tonight? I need your help to study for the physiology exam.
7. The victim finally came into **view** when the sun started to rise.
8. This first-aid kit comes **complete** with adhesive bandages, antiseptic wipes and a first-aid manual.
9. I'll come **right** back with your medication.
10. The firefighter came to my **rescue** when I was trapped in a burning building.

P.36

Exercise 7

Conversation 1

A. Good morning Mrs Jones. Thank you for coming.

B. Hello doctor. Why did you want to see me?

A. Your test results have come back.

B. And?

A. It's not good news I'm afraid.

B. Oh well. Luckily, I came mentally prepared for bad news.

A. There are some treatment options. Let's talk about them and come to a decision.

Conversation 2

A. I went to see the doctor this morning. He gave me bad news about my condition. He told me to discuss it with you and come to an agreement together.

B. Sure.

A. Now that my life is coming to an end, I've decided not to have any further treatment.

B. Oh.

A. I've come to the realization that I'd like to die at home with my family rather than in a hospital.

B. I don't think I can come to terms with that decision. Can't we come to a compromise?

A. No, sorry. Please respect my decision.

P.36

Exercise 8

Example answers.

1. Enter!
2. The soldiers came under fire.
3. I couldn't think of any ways to lose weight.
4. The monster in the horror movie revived.
5. I can't agree with your decision.

P.37

Exercise 10

Example answers

1. Do you need to come to a decision?

I need to decide about my future.

2. Do you need to come clean about anything?

I need to tell my wife about my gambling addiction.

3. What would you like to come to an end?

I would like coffee shops and restaurants to stop using plastic straws.

4. Who or what comes first in your life?

My kids and my wife come first.

5. Have you ever come a cropper?

I once broke my leg when I was skiing.

UNIT 7 GET

P.39

Exercise 2

1. Have you got an **appointment**?
2. Don't get so **upset**, it's only a small mistake.
3. Can you get me a glass of **water**, please?
4. I couldn't get out of bed this **morning**.
5. I've got the flu, please get me some **medicine**.
6. You can't come in. You need to get **permission**.
7. My **uncle** is getting old and he has no one to look after him.
8. Get out of the car and go inside the **house**.
9. **Winter** is coming, it's getting colder.
10. I'll get you a **chair**, stand here for a moment.

P.39

Exercise 3

1.C 2.E 3.A 4.G 5.H 6.F 7.D 8.B 9.I 10.J

P.40

Exercise 4

1. You need to get this before you can drive a car. You need a **driving license**.
2. It takes me longer to do things these days. I must be getting **old**.
3. My wound is dirty, it got **Infected**.
4. I danced. **I got down.**
5. She is crying. She got **upset**.
6. I need a cup of coffee. I'm getting **tired**.
7. I need to go to the pharmacy to get my **prescription**.
8. Leave my house, now! **Get out**!
9. Turn on the heater. I'm getting **cold**.
10. I haven't gotten the flu so far this year. I haven't gotten **sick**.

P.40

Exercise 5

Example answers

1. I got sick last week, but I'm okay now.
2. I didn't get up in time for my doctor's appointment.
3. I need to get my prescription refilled.
4. I've never gotten any serious injuries.
5. I want to get my license to practice medicine.
6. She is getting cranky. Give her something to eat.
7. It hasn't got any restrooms. You should go before we arrive.
8. They like to get everything done at the start of their shift.
9. Can you get me the patient's chart, please?
10. I don't have time to get sick. I'm too busy.

P.41

Exercise 6

1. A. warm 2. B. top 3. C. out of air 4. B. deaf drunk 5. D. clothed 6. D. permit

P.41

Exercise 7

1. A. I will come to visit you tomorrow. Is there anything you need?
2. B. Yes, could you get me a few things from the supermarket?
3. A. Sure. What would you like?
4. B. Please, get me some snacks.
5. A. Okay. Snacks got it.
6. B. Could you also get me a small bottle of whisky?
7. A. I don't think that's a good idea. I don't want to get in trouble. Did you get permission from your doctor?
8. B. I will ask her, but I don't think she will let me get drunk while I'm in hospital.
9. A. Is there anything else? It's getting dark, I want to get your things then get home before it gets too late.
10. B. No, that's all thank you. You should get off.

P.42

Exercise 8

a headache / a cold / hurt / annoyed / frightened / sick / fit / into trouble / pregnant / a shock

P.42

Exercise 10

Example answers

1. What time do you usually get up?

I usually get up at half-past six in the morning.

2. When was the last time you got sick?

I caught the flu last month.

3. What gets you down?

I get depressed when my favourite soccer team loses.

4. Who do you get along with?

I get along with all of my co-workers.

5. What would you like to get into?

I would like to get into a new yoga.

UNIT 8 REVIEW

P.43

Exercise 1

Bring	Come	Get
life	to terms with	up
up	early	off
off	up	back
back	off	down
to mind	back	closer
down	to mind	angry
change	down	divorced
closer	to a decision	married
to an end	closer	a cold
together	to an end	sick
out	together	together
over	last	lost
to a head	out	out
forth	over	over
in	to a head	in
	alive	
	forth	
	in	

P.43

Exercise 2

1. The doctors **came** to an agreement about which medication to prescribe to the patient.
2. The professor always **brings** out the best in his medical students.
3. The procedure **gets** bad press, but it is effective.
4. My internship at this hospital is **coming** to an end.
5. Can you **come** closer? My eyes aren't what they used to be.
6. I'm afraid I've **got** bad news about your husband.
7. There is no need to **get** angry. Please, calm down.
8. When you **get** the chance, please make an appointment to see me.

P.44

Exercise 3

1.K 2.B 3.D 4.C 5.E 6.H 7.F 8.G 9.L 10.I 11.A 12.J

P.44

Exercise 4

1. My wife brought up her breakfast this morning.
2. I brought her to hospital
3. I was worried that she had gotten sick.
4. The doctor told me that she had gotten pregnant.
5. After hearing the news, an uneasy feeling came over me.
6. I asked when she might have gotten into this condition.
7. I got shocked by his answer.
8. I had gotten sent to prison at that time.
9. I'm not sure what I will do when the baby comes.
10. We might get divorced.
11. I might bring it up as if it was my own.
12. I must come to a decision.

P.44

Exercise 5

Example answers

1. Would you like to come with me to visit grandma in hospital tomorrow?
2. Please, bring the patient's chart to the meeting.
3. Can you get me some sterile examination gloves, please?
4. I've got a terrible headache.
5. I would like to get fitter.
6. I wouldn't like to get any more stress.

P.45

Exercise 6

1. I brought some medical students with me to observe, is that okay?
2. Can you come a little closer? I need to examine you.
3. When did you get this? It looks infected.
4. How did you get this? It looks painful.
5. When I came, no one was here, so I went to a different clinic.
6. I need you to get some sedatives for this patient as soon as possible.

P.45

Exercise 7

1. Bring up to date

To renew or to share current information.

2. Bring to one's senses

To resume acting normally or sensibly.

3. Come back to haunt one

To cause problems in the future.

P.45

Exercise 8

1. Q. <u>What time did you get here?</u>

A. I got here at twelve o'clock. You were sleeping when I came.

2. Q. <u>Can you get me a coffee?</u>

A. Sure. Would you like milk and sugar?

3. Q. <u>What brought you to see me today?</u>

A. I have a sore throat and a fever.

UNIT 9 FEEL

P.48

Exercise 2

1. Feel nervous
2. Feel upset
3. Feel annoyed
4. Feel pity
5. No hard feelings
6. Strong feelings
7. Feel deeply
8. Feel like a beer
9. Feel dizzy
10. Feel okay

P.48

Exercise 3

1. The patient's skin **<u>felt</u>** cold.
2. The patient is **<u>feeling</u>** terrible because of the pain.
3. He has been **<u>feeling</u>** like death for a long time.
4. She **<u>felt</u>** someone touch her arm.
5. I **<u>felt</u>** a flash of pain when the man punched me in the face.
6. I can't **<u>feel</u>** a pulse.
7. Who is **<u>feeling</u>** unwell?
8. Can you **<u>feel</u>** this?
9. You've hurt his **<u>feelings</u>**.
10. I'm **<u>feeling</u>** good.

P.48

Exercise 4

<u>pessimistic</u> <u>inferior</u> (confident) (optimistic) <u>jealousy</u>

(joy) (content) (proud) <u>hatred</u> <u>anxious</u>

P.49

Exercise 5

Example answers

1. I'm feeling confident about my exam results.
2. She is feeling optimistic.
3. I felt an extreme sense of joy when my daughter was born.
4. He feels content with his life.
5. I don't feel very proud of what I've done.
6. There is no need to feel so pessimistic.
7. Are you feeling anxious about flying?
8. I feel inferior to my older brother.
9. She feels only hate towards her ex-husband.
10. Everyone feels jealous when they see him.

P.49

Exercise 6

Example answers

1. I've been feeling lonely since my wife left me.
2. I felt relieved when I got my test results back.
3. I can't do this. I feel overwhelmed.
4. He is feeling resentful of his ex-wife. She took everything in the divorce.
5. The chairs in the waiting room feel quite uncomfortable.
6. Leave him alone. Can't you see he is feeling irritated?
7. I've been feeling insecure since I got a low score in the IQ test.
8. He has been feeling more energetic since he started taking multivitamins every morning.
9. Why don't you feel ashamed? You are a disgrace.
10. I felt a little hopeful when I heard the news.

P.50

Exercise 7

1. How does Jim feel?

He has been feeling blue.

2. Why did Jim's wife leave him?

She left him because she hadn't been feeling like herself.

3. How does Jim's wife feel now?

She feels like a new woman.

4. What shouldn't Jim do?

He shouldn't drink alcohol.

5. What advice does the therapist give?

He could try to get some exercise, go on a date or take up a new hobby.

6. When can Jim contact the therapist?

Anytime.

P.51

Exercise 8

Example answer

Dear Dr Jones,

I've been feeling really stressed at work. My boss and I haven't been getting along. In fact, his feelings towards me seem to have changed. I think he feels resentful about my success. I haven't been sleeping well either, so I've been feeling exhausted every day. I've been drinking a lot of coffee to help me feel alive in the mornings. I'm really confused about this. I don't know how to feel or what to do.

Thanks.

Bob.

P.51

Exercise 10

Example answers

1. How are you feeling right now?

I'm feeling calm and relaxed.

2. What do you do if a patient is feeling bored?

I start a conversation with them.

3. What makes you feel blue?

I feel blue when I fail a test.

4. What makes you feel angry?

People who drive badly make me feel angry.

5. What makes you feel terrified?

The thought of being alone in my old age terrifies me.

UNIT 10 HAVE

P.52

Exercise 2

1.B 2.C 3.E 4.D 5.G 6.F 7.A 8.I 9.J 10.H

P.52

Exercise 3

Example answers

1. I've been throwing up and I have terrible diarrhea. I must have food **poisoning**.
2. My wife is pregnant. We are going to have a **baby**.
3. When would you like to have your next **appointment**?
4. My mother is 80 years old, she can't remember things. She has **dementia**.
5. I'm dirty and smelly, I need to have a **bath**.
6. We need to have a serious talk. Let's have a **discussion**.
7. At least try it. You need to have a **go**.
8. I'm feeling a little sleepy. I'm going to have a **nap**.
9. Please, help me. I'm having a little **trouble**.
10. Please send an ambulance, my husband has had an **accident**.

P.54

Exercise 4

1. I **had** a cold last week. I **had** to take some medicine.
2. James is exhausted he needs to **have** a rest.
3. She can't afford to take a taxi to the hospital. She doesn't **have** any money.
4. My grandmother **has** Alzheimer's disease. She gets confused easily. I think she will **have** to move into a nursing home.
5. I've been **having** trouble sleeping recently. Last night I **had** a nightmare about zombies.
6. Do you **have** an appointment? We are **having** problems with our PC, so I can't check the schedule.
7. What **have** you eaten today? I **had** a sandwich.
8. My wife **had** a baby last week, but I **haven't** met him yet.
9. He **has** a lot of work to do, but he doesn't **have** enough time.
10. **Have** you seen my husband? He was taken to hospital this morning. I think he might **have had** a heart attack. He **has** brown hair and green eyes.

P.54 & 55

Exercise 5

1. Why did James visit the counsellor?

He has been having problems with his wife.

2. What has James' wife been doing that upset James?

She has been yelling at him.

3. How has James been feeling?

He has been feeling lonely.

4. How is James' hygiene?

It's not very good. He has bad breath.

5. What is James' problem?

James has a drinking problem.

6. What should James do?

He should join the therapy group for alcoholics.

P.55

Exercise 6

Example answers

1. I had an argument with my boss.
2. You need to have a shower, you smell terrible.
3. Why don't you have a go at therapy? You should talk about your problems with a professional.
4. I have never broken a bone even though I play a lot of sports.

P.55

Exercise 7

1. My cat had **kittens / puppies / cubs** yesterday. We are having a little **easy / trouble / problems** looking after them.
2. I have put on **weight / fat / heavy** recently. I have to **start / continue / stop** eating junk food.
3. I have twelve patients to look after in my ward. I'm going to have a **crowded / busy / easy** day tomorrow.
4. Bob has to go to **hospital / home / prison** for three years, before now he had never been in **trouble / problems / difficulty** with the law.
5. The president of the company had a major heart **assault / stroke / attack**. He has to have heart **surgery / operation / procedure**.

P.56

Exercise 8

1. have cold feet

To be anxious about something you plan to do.

2. have a big head

To believe you are important or to be arrogant.

P.56

Exercise 10

Example answers

1. What do you do if you have a headache?

I take some pain killers and have a nap.

2. Have you been sick recently?

No, I haven't'. The last time I was sick was last year.

3. Do you have any regrets?

I wish I'd studied English harder in school.

4. How have you been?

I've been a little stressed.

5. What responsibilities do you have at work?

I am responsible for administering medication to patients.

UNIT 11 MAKE

P.58

Exercise 2

1.A 2.B 3.A 4.B 5.B 6.B 7.B 8.A 9.B 10.C

P.58

Exercise 3

1.D H 2.I 3.J 4.D H 5.E 6.F 7.G 8.B 9.C 10.A

P.59

Exercise 4

1. better, well, healthy
2. sick, tired
3. mess
4. happy
5. appointment
6. take
7. life
8. better, well, healthy
9. mistake
10. baby

P.60

Exercise 5

1.O 2.D 3.C 4.A 5.H 6.F 7.G 8.E 9.L 10.J

P.60

Exercise 6

Example answers

What makes you happy?

Spending time with my family makes me happy.

What makes you sad?

Being alone on my birthday makes me feel a little sad.

What makes you angry?

People who interrupt me when I'm speaking make me angry.

P.61

Exercise 7

1. Why did Bobby cry?

He was in an accident.

2. Why couldn't the parents pay for a taxi or health insurance?

They didn't make enough money.

3. How did they get to the hospital?

We don't know. They made their own way. They didn't take a taxi.

4. Who made an effort to help?

A nurse and her rich friend.

5. Was Bobby okay in the end?

No, he wasn't. He died.

P.61

Exercise 8

Example answer

Last year I broke my back when I was snowboarding. I tried to do a jump but didn't quite make it. I crashed and landed badly on my back. I hadn't made the effort to buy any protective gear. I made it to my feet and slowly made my way down the mountain. I made it back to my car. Finally, I made it home, my wife made a great effort to help me. We went to the hospital and the doctors made me take an x-ray, MRI and CT. My vertebrae had been fractured so the hospital made a special corset for me to wear. After seven months I made a full recovery.

P.62

Exercise 10

Example answers

1. If you make someone upset, how can you make it up to them?

I might buy them flowers or chocolates.

2. Your friend is depressed. How can you make them happy?

I would take them out to a bar or restaurant and try to make them have a good time.

3. What can you make well?

I can make a very good omelette.

4. You have a cold. What can you do to make yourself better?

I buy medicine from the drug store and rest as much as possible.

5. How do you make a traditional remedy in your country?

I make chicken noodle soup. I make it with chicken breast, chicken broth, vegetables and egg noodles.

UNIT 12 REVIEW

P.63

Exercise 1

D	I	F	F	E	R	E	N	C	E	P	L	A	N	S
I								N						Y
S								A						M
E			M			W	O	U	N	D				P
A			A					S						A
S	I	C	K					E						T
E		O	E			T		O			P			H
		M				I		U			R			Y
		P	R	O	G	R	E	S	S		O			
		L				E				A	B	O	U	T
	H	A	V	E		D	O	W	N		L			H
	F	I					C				E			O
	E	N		A	P	P	O	I	N	T	M	E	N	T
B	E	T	T	E	R		L							
	L						D							

P.64

Exercise 2

1. feel good 2. make a confession 3. have a backache 4. feel sorry 5. make a discovery 6. feel funny 7. feel concerned 8. have a stroke 9. make an excuse 10. make an exception

P.64

Exercise 3

Example answers

1. I'm feeling good for the first time in a long while.
2. I have a confession to make. I kissed your wife.
3. I can't go skiing because I have a backache.
4. Don't feel sorry for me. I'm fine.
5. Who made the greatest medical discovery of all time?
6. I feel kind of funny.
7. Do you feel concerned about Bob?
8. Joe's father-in-law had a stroke.
9. Don't make any more excuses, I don't want to hear them.
10. We can't make any exceptions.

P.65

Exercise 4

1. better 2. sandwich 3. pass 4. plans 5. hate 6. fortune 7. discovery 8. bath 9. baby 10. operation

P.65

Exercise 5

1. He is having a panic attack.
2. She shouldn't have to work so hard in her condition.
3. Bob had a fight with a man in a pub.
4. He had to strain when he was having a poo.
5. My wife hasn't talked to me since we had a row.
6. Who made this mess?
7. I've been having nightmares every night for a week.
8. Bob must be feeling lonely because he doesn't have any friends.
9. How do you feel now that you have a licence to practice medicine?
10. Who feels like making me a snack?

P.66

Exercise 6

Example answers

1. I'm married.
I have a wife.
2. Bob baked a cake for his mother's birthday.
Bob made a cake for his mother's birthday.
3. How are you today?
How are you feeling today?
4. Does your stomach hurt?
Do you have a stomachache?
5. How is the medicine affecting you?
How does the medicine make you feel?
6. The medicine isn't working.
The medicine isn't making any difference.
7. We need to talk about the patient's treatment.
We need to have a discussion about the patient's treatment.
8. My dog is limping. He might have a thorn in his paw.
My dog has a limp. He might have a thorn in his paw.
9. Try to get along better with your co-workers after the argument.
Try to make friends with your co-workers after the argument.
10. You need to lose some weight. Eat a salad once in a while.
You have to lose some weight. Have a salad once in a while.

P.66

Exercise 7

1. I **have** a lisp it is difficult for me to pronounce S sounds.
2. He doesn't **have** a passion for life anymore.
3. The bully **made** fun of the smaller boy.
4. Are you **feeling** anxious about having a baby?
5. Milk doesn't agree with me. It makes me **feel** sick.
6. I don't **have** any love for her anymore.

P.67

Exercise 8

Example answer

D. What made you come to see me today?

P. I've been throwing up every hour since yesterday morning.

D. I see. Have you had any unusual food lately?

P. I haven't had anything strange at all.

D. How have you been feeling in your daily life?

P. I've been feeling anxious.

D. Maybe your physical symptoms have to do with stress. Try having a rest.

P. Can I have some medicine?

D. Not until I have made a full diagnosis.

P. I understand. Have a nice day doctor.

D. You too. I hope you feel better.

Notes

Notes

Visit www.premierpotentialpublishing.com for information about other textbooks from Premier Potential Publishing.

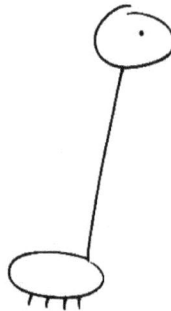

Premier Potential Publishing

www.ingramcontent.com/pod-product-compliance
Lightning Source LLC
Chambersburg PA
CBHW062113090426
42741CB00016B/3405
* 9 7 8 4 9 9 1 0 6 0 0 5 2 *